Welcome to your Joy Journal

This journal is designed for you to move into a higher vibrational state through a daily or weekly joyful reflection. Be kind to yourself if you forget to write, the pages of this book will still be here for you.

Why I bought this journal

_____
_____

I hope at the end of this book, I ...

_____
_____

Joy can be found in the smallest things

Daily Joys

Date: _____

I see joy in myself when...

_____
_____
_____

I see joy in others when...

_____
_____
_____

I see joy in the world when...

_____
_____
_____

You have permission to be joyful

Daily Joys

Date: _____

I see joy in myself when...

_____
_____
_____

I see joy in others when...

_____
_____
_____

I see joy in the world when...

_____
_____
_____

You have permission to be joyful

Daily Joys

Date: _____

I see joy in myself when...

_____
_____
_____

I see joy in others when...

_____
_____
_____

I see joy in the world when...

_____
_____
_____

You have permission to be joyful

Daily Joys

Date: _____

I see joy in myself when...

_____
_____
_____

I see joy in others when...

_____
_____
_____

I see joy in the world when...

_____
_____
_____

You have permission to be joyful

Daily Joys

Date: _____

I see joy in myself when...

_____
_____
_____

I see joy in others when...

_____
_____
_____

I see joy in the world when...

_____
_____
_____

You have permission to
be joyful

Daily Joys

Date: _____

I see joy in myself when...

_____
_____
_____

I see joy in others when...

_____
_____
_____

I see joy in the world when...

_____
_____
_____

You have permission to be joyful

Daily Joys

Date: _____

I see joy in myself when...

_____
_____
_____

I see joy in others when...

_____
_____
_____

I see joy in the world when...

_____
_____
_____

You have permission to
be joyful

Daily Joys

Date: _____

I see joy in myself when...

_____
_____
_____

I see joy in others when...

_____
_____
_____

I see joy in the world when...

_____
_____
_____

You have permission to be joyful

Daily Joys

Date: _____

I see joy in myself when...
_____
_____
_____

I see joy in others when...
_____
_____
_____

I see joy in the world when...
_____
_____
_____

You have permission to be joyful

Daily Joys

Date: _____

I see joy in myself when...

_____
_____
_____

I see joy in others when...

_____
_____
_____

I see joy in the world when...

_____
_____
_____

You have permission to be joyful

Daily Joys

Date: _____

I see joy in myself when...

_____
_____
_____

I see joy in others when...

_____
_____
_____

I see joy in the world when...

_____
_____
_____

You have permission to
be joyful

Daily Joys

Date: _____

I see joy in myself when...

_____
_____
_____

I see joy in others when...

_____
_____
_____

I see joy in the world when...

_____
_____
_____

You have permission to
be joyful

Daily Joys

Date: _____

I see joy in myself when...

_____
_____
_____

I see joy in others when...

_____
_____
_____

I see joy in the world when...

_____
_____
_____

You have permission to be joyful

Daily Joys

Date: _____

I see joy in myself when...

_____
_____
_____

I see joy in others when...

_____
_____
_____

I see joy in the world when...

_____
_____
_____

You have permission to
be joyful

Daily Joys

Date: _____

I see joy in myself when...

_____
_____
_____

I see joy in others when...

_____
_____
_____

I see joy in the world when...

_____
_____
_____

You have permission to
be joyful

Daily Joys

Date: _____

I see joy in myself when...

_____
_____
_____

I see joy in others when...

_____
_____
_____

I see joy in the world when...

_____
_____
_____

You have permission to
be joyful

Daily Joys

Date: _____

I see joy in myself when...

_____
_____
_____

I see joy in others when...

_____
_____
_____

I see joy in the world when...

_____
_____
_____

You have permission to
be joyful

Daily Joys

Date: _____

I see joy in myself when...

_____
_____
_____

I see joy in others when...

_____
_____
_____

I see joy in the world when...

_____
_____
_____

You have permission to be joyful

Daily Joys

Date: _____

I see joy in myself when...

_____
_____
_____

I see joy in others when...

_____
_____
_____

I see joy in the world when...

_____
_____
_____

You have permission to
be joyful

Daily Joys

Date: _____

I see joy in myself when...

_____
_____
_____

I see joy in others when...

_____
_____
_____

I see joy in the world when...

_____
_____
_____

You have permission to be joyful

Daily Joys

Date: _____

I see joy in myself when...

_____
_____
_____

I see joy in others when...

_____
_____
_____

I see joy in the world when...

_____
_____
_____

You have permission to be joyful

Daily Joys

Date: _____

I see joy in myself when...
_____
_____
_____

I see joy in others when...
_____
_____
_____

I see joy in the world when...
_____
_____
_____

You have permission to be joyful

Daily Joys

Date: _____

I see joy in myself when...

_____
_____
_____

I see joy in others when...

_____
_____
_____

I see joy in the world when...

_____
_____
_____

You have permission to
be joyful

Daily Joys

Date: _____

I see joy in myself when...

_____
_____
_____

I see joy in others when...

_____
_____
_____

I see joy in the world when...

_____
_____
_____

You have permission to
be joyful

Daily Joys

Date: _____

I see joy in myself when...

_____
_____
_____

I see joy in others when...

_____
_____
_____

I see joy in the world when...

_____
_____
_____

You have permission to
be joyful

Daily Joys

Date: _____

I see joy in myself when...

_____
_____
_____

I see joy in others when...

_____
_____
_____

I see joy in the world when...

_____
_____
_____

You have permission to be joyful

Daily Joys

Date: _____

I see joy in myself when...

_____
_____
_____

I see joy in others when...

_____
_____
_____

I see joy in the world when...

_____
_____
_____

You have permission to be joyful

Daily Joys

Date: _____

I see joy in myself when...

_____
_____
_____

I see joy in others when...

_____
_____
_____

I see joy in the world when...

_____
_____
_____

You have permission to be joyful

Daily Joys

Date: _____

I see joy in myself when...

_____
_____
_____

I see joy in others when...

_____
_____
_____

I see joy in the world when...

_____
_____
_____

You have permission to be joyful

Daily Joys

Date: _____

I see joy in myself when...

_____
_____
_____

I see joy in others when...

_____
_____
_____

I see joy in the world when...

_____
_____
_____

You have permission to be joyful

Daily Joys

Date: _____

I see joy in myself when...

_____
_____
_____

I see joy in others when...

_____
_____
_____

I see joy in the world when...

_____
_____
_____

You have permission to be joyful

Daily Joys

Date: _____

I see joy in myself when...

_____
_____
_____

I see joy in others when...

_____
_____
_____

I see joy in the world when...

_____
_____
_____

You have permission to be joyful

Daily Joys

Date: _____

I see joy in myself when…

_____
_____
_____

I see joy in others when…

_____
_____
_____

I see joy in the world when…

_____
_____
_____

You have permission to
be joyful

Daily Joys

Date: _____

I see joy in myself when...

_____
_____
_____

I see joy in others when...

_____
_____
_____

I see joy in the world when...

_____
_____
_____

You have permission to be joyful

Daily Joys

Date: _____

I see joy in myself when...

_____
_____
_____

I see joy in others when...

_____
_____
_____

I see joy in the world when...

_____
_____
_____

You have permission to
be joyful

Daily Joys

Date: _____

I see joy in myself when...

_____
_____
_____

I see joy in others when...

_____
_____
_____

I see joy in the world when...

_____
_____
_____

You have permission to be joyful

Daily Joys

Date: _____

I see joy in myself when...

_____
_____
_____

I see joy in others when...

_____
_____
_____

I see joy in the world when...

_____
_____
_____

You have permission to be joyful

Daily Joys

Date: _____

I see joy in myself when...

_____
_____
_____

I see joy in others when...

_____
_____
_____

I see joy in the world when...

_____
_____
_____

You have permission to be joyful

Daily Joys

Date: _____

I see joy in myself when...

_____
_____
_____

I see joy in others when...

_____
_____
_____

I see joy in the world when...

_____
_____
_____

You have permission to be joyful

Daily Joys

Date: _____

I see joy in myself when...

_____
_____
_____

I see joy in others when...

_____
_____
_____

I see joy in the world when...

_____
_____
_____

You have permission to be joyful

Daily Joys

Date: _____

I see joy in myself when...
_____
_____
_____

I see joy in others when...
_____
_____
_____

I see joy in the world when...
_____
_____
_____

You have permission to
be joyful

Daily Joys

Date: _____

I see joy in myself when...

_____
_____
_____

I see joy in others when...

_____
_____
_____

I see joy in the world when...

_____
_____

You have permission to be joyful

Daily Joys

Date: _____

I see joy in myself when…

_____
_____
_____

I see joy in others when…

_____
_____
_____

I see joy in the world when…

_____
_____
_____

You have permission to
be joyful

Daily Joys

Date: _____

I see joy in myself when...

_____
_____
_____

I see joy in others when...

_____
_____
_____

I see joy in the world when...

_____
_____
_____

You have permission to be joyful

Daily Joys

Date: _____

I see joy in myself when...

_____
_____
_____

I see joy in others when...

_____
_____
_____

I see joy in the world when...

_____
_____
_____

You have permission to
be joyful

Daily Joys

Date: _____

I see joy in myself when...

_____
_____
_____

I see joy in others when...

_____
_____
_____

I see joy in the world when...

_____
_____
_____

You have permission to be joyful

Daily Joys

Date: _____

I see joy in myself when...

_____
_____
_____

I see joy in others when...

_____
_____
_____

I see joy in the world when...

_____
_____
_____

You have permission to
be joyful

Daily Joys

Date: _____

I see joy in myself when…

_____
_____
_____

I see joy in others when…

_____
_____
_____

I see joy in the world when…

_____
_____
_____

You have permission to be joyful

Daily Joys

Date: _____

I see joy in myself when...

_____
_____
_____

I see joy in others when...

_____
_____
_____

I see joy in the world when...

_____
_____
_____

You have permission to be joyful

Daily Joys

Date: _____

I see joy in myself when...

_____
_____
_____

I see joy in others when...

_____
_____
_____

I see joy in the world when...

_____
_____
_____

You have permission to be joyful

Daily Joys

Date: _____

I see joy in myself when...

_____
_____
_____

I see joy in others when...

_____
_____
_____

I see joy in the world when...

_____
_____
_____

You have permission to be joyful

Daily Joys

Date: _____

I see joy in myself when...

_____
_____
_____

I see joy in others when...

_____
_____
_____

I see joy in the world when...

_____
_____
_____

You have permission to be joyful

Daily Joys

Date: _____

I see joy in myself when...
_____
_____
_____

I see joy in others when...
_____
_____
_____

I see joy in the world when...
_____
_____
_____

You have permission to
be joyful

Daily Joys

Date: _____

I see joy in myself when...

_____
_____
_____

I see joy in others when...

_____
_____
_____

I see joy in the world when...

_____
_____
_____

You have permission to
be joyful

Daily Joys

Date: _____

I see joy in myself when...

_____
_____
_____

I see joy in others when...

_____
_____
_____

I see joy in the world when...

_____
_____
_____

You have permission to
be joyful

Daily Joys

Date: _____

I see joy in myself when…

_____
_____
_____

I see joy in others when…

_____
_____
_____

I see joy in the world when…

_____
_____
_____

You have permission to
be joyful

Daily Joys

Date: _____

I see joy in myself when...

_____
_____
_____

I see joy in others when...

_____
_____
_____

I see joy in the world when...

_____
_____
_____

You have permission to
be joyful

Daily Joys

Date: _____

I see joy in myself when...
_____
_____
_____

I see joy in others when...
_____
_____
_____

I see joy in the world when...
_____
_____
_____

You have permission to be joyful

Daily Joys

Date: _____

I see joy in myself when...

_____
_____
_____

I see joy in others when...

_____
_____
_____

I see joy in the world when...

_____
_____
_____

You have permission to be joyful

Daily Joys

Date: _____

I see joy in myself when...

_____
_____
_____

I see joy in others when...

_____
_____
_____

I see joy in the world when...

_____
_____
_____

You have permission to be joyful

Daily Joys

Date: _____

I see joy in myself when...
_____
_____
_____

I see joy in others when...
_____
_____
_____

I see joy in the world when...
_____
_____
_____

You have permission to be joyful

Daily Joys

Date: _____

I see joy in myself when...

_____
_____
_____

I see joy in others when...

_____
_____
_____

I see joy in the world when...

_____
_____
_____

You have permission to be joyful

Daily Joys

Date: _____

I see joy in myself when...
_____
_____
_____

I see joy in others when...
_____
_____
_____

I see joy in the world when...
_____
_____
_____

You have permission to
be joyful

Daily Joys

Date: _____

I see joy in myself when...
_____
_____
_____

I see joy in others when...
_____
_____
_____

I see joy in the world when...
_____
_____
_____

You have permission to be joyful

Daily Joys

Date: _____

I see joy in myself when...

_____
_____
_____

I see joy in others when...

_____
_____
_____

I see joy in the world when...

_____
_____
_____

You have permission to
be joyful

Daily Joys

Date: _____

I see joy in myself when...

_____
_____
_____

I see joy in others when...

_____
_____
_____

I see joy in the world when...

_____
_____
_____

You have permission to
be joyful

Daily Joys

Date: _____

I see joy in myself when...

_____
_____
_____

I see joy in others when...

_____
_____
_____

I see joy in the world when...

_____
_____
_____

You have permission to be joyful

Daily Joys

Date: _____

I see joy in myself when...

_____
_____
_____

I see joy in others when...

_____
_____
_____

I see joy in the world when...

_____
_____
_____

You have permission to be joyful

Daily Joys

Date: _____

I see joy in myself when...

_____
_____
_____

I see joy in others when...

_____
_____
_____

I see joy in the world when...

_____
_____
_____

You have permission to be joyful

Daily Joys

Date: _____

I see joy in myself when...

_____
_____
_____

I see joy in others when...

_____
_____
_____

I see joy in the world when...

_____
_____
_____

You have permission to be joyful

Daily Joys

Date: _____

I see joy in myself when...
_____
_____
_____

I see joy in others when...
_____
_____
_____

I see joy in the world when...
_____
_____
_____

You have permission to be joyful

Daily Joys

Date: _____

I see joy in myself when...

_____
_____
_____

I see joy in others when...

_____
_____
_____

I see joy in the world when...

_____
_____
_____

You have permission to be joyful

Daily Joys

Date: _____

I see joy in myself when...
_____
_____
_____

I see joy in others when...
_____
_____
_____

I see joy in the world when...
_____
_____
_____

You have permission to be joyful

Daily Joys

Date: _____

I see joy in myself when…

_____
_____
_____

I see joy in others when…

_____
_____
_____

I see joy in the world when…

_____
_____
_____

You have permission to
be joyful

Daily Joys

Date: _____

I see joy in myself when...

_____
_____
_____

I see joy in others when...

_____
_____
_____

I see joy in the world when...

_____
_____

You have permission to
be joyful

Daily Joys

Date: _____

I see joy in myself when...

_____
_____
_____

I see joy in others when...

_____
_____
_____

I see joy in the world when...

_____
_____
_____

You have permission to be joyful

Daily Joys

Date: _____

I see joy in myself when...
_____
_____
_____

I see joy in others when...
_____
_____
_____

I see joy in the world when...
_____
_____
_____

You have permission to
be joyful

Daily Joys

Date: _____

I see joy in myself when...

_____
_____
_____

I see joy in others when...

_____
_____
_____

I see joy in the world when...

_____
_____
_____

You have permission to be joyful

Daily Joys

Date: _____

I see joy in myself when...

_____
_____
_____

I see joy in others when...

_____
_____
_____

I see joy in the world when...

_____
_____
_____

You have permission to
be joyful

Daily Joys

Date: _____

I see joy in myself when...

_____
_____
_____

I see joy in others when...

_____
_____
_____

I see joy in the world when...

_____
_____
_____

You have permission to
be joyful

Daily Joys

Date: _____

I see joy in myself when...
_____
_____
_____

I see joy in others when...
_____
_____
_____

I see joy in the world when...
_____
_____
_____

You have permission to
be joyful

Daily Joys

Date: _____

I see joy in myself when...

_____
_____
_____

I see joy in others when...

_____
_____
_____

I see joy in the world when...

_____
_____
_____

You have permission to be joyful

Daily Joys

Date: _____

I see joy in myself when...
_____
_____
_____

I see joy in others when...
_____
_____
_____

I see joy in the world when...
_____
_____
_____

You have permission to be joyful

Daily Joys

Date: _____

I see joy in myself when...

_____
_____
_____

I see joy in others when...

_____
_____
_____

I see joy in the world when...

_____
_____
_____

You have permission to be joyful

Daily Joys

Date: _____

I see joy in myself when...

_____
_____
_____

I see joy in others when...

_____
_____
_____

I see joy in the world when...

_____
_____
_____

You have permission to
be joyful

Daily Joys

Date: _____

I see joy in myself when...

_____
_____
_____

I see joy in others when...

_____
_____
_____

I see joy in the world when...

_____
_____
_____

You have permission to
be joyful

Daily Joys

Date: _____

I see joy in myself when...
_____
_____
_____

I see joy in others when...
_____
_____
_____

I see joy in the world when...
_____
_____
_____

You have permission to
be joyful

Daily Joys

Date: _____

I see joy in myself when...

_____
_____
_____

I see joy in others when...

_____
_____
_____

I see joy in the world when...

_____
_____
_____

You have permission to be joyful

Daily Joys

Date: _____

I see joy in myself when...

_____
_____
_____

I see joy in others when...

_____
_____
_____

I see joy in the world when...

_____
_____
_____

You have permission to
be joyful

Daily Joys

Date: _____

I see joy in myself when...

_____
_____
_____

I see joy in others when...

_____
_____
_____

I see joy in the world when...

_____
_____
_____

You have permission to be joyful

Daily Joys

Date: _____

I see joy in myself when...

_____
_____
_____

I see joy in others when...

_____
_____
_____

I see joy in the world when...

_____
_____
_____

You have permission to be joyful

Daily Joys

Date: _____

I see joy in myself when...

_____
_____
_____

I see joy in others when...

_____
_____
_____

I see joy in the world when...

_____
_____
_____

You have permission to be joyful

Daily Joys

Date: _____

I see joy in myself when...

_____
_____
_____

I see joy in others when...

_____
_____
_____

I see joy in the world when...

_____
_____
_____

You have permission to
be joyful

Daily Joys

Date: _____

I see joy in myself when...

_____
_____
_____

I see joy in others when...

_____
_____
_____

I see joy in the world when...

_____
_____
_____

You have permission to be joyful

Daily Joys

Date: _____

I see joy in myself when...

_____
_____
_____

I see joy in others when...

_____
_____
_____

I see joy in the world when...

_____
_____
_____

You have permission to
be joyful

Joyful reflection

Date: _____

Return to the start and re-read your previous entries
_____
_____
_____

Do you notice any recurring themes or ideas?
_____
_____
_____

What were you surprised by?
_____
_____
_____

Spread joy like confetti

The final page

This practice has taught me

_____
_____
_____

This is not the end, this is just the beginning...

I am joyful

Rising Spirit
WHERE GREAT IDEAS GROW

All rights reserved. No part of this book may be used or reproduced by any means, graphic, electronic, or mechanical, including photocopying, recording, taping or by any information storage retrieval system without the written permission of the copyright owner.
Published in Australia by Rising Spirit; Where Great Ideas Grow and Alyssa Curtayne, © 2023.

I am joyful

www.ingramcontent.com/pod-product-compliance
Lightning Source LLC
Chambersburg PA
CBHW040243010526

44107CB00065B/2855